Contents

READING SKILLS 2
   Speed reading strategies for comprehension 2
   What to look for in texts 3
   Annotation strategies 4
   Understanding evidence in texts 5
   Dissecting questions 6
   Word-level close analysis 7

WRITING SKILLS 8

Analytical writing skills 8
   Essay structure 8
   Sentence starters for essay writing 9
   Integrating quotes 10
   Comparative analysis 11
   Foundational techniques 12
   Advanced techniques 14

Imaginative writing skills 16
   Key strategies 16
   Show, don't tell 17
   Sensory descriptions 18
   Point of view (POV) perspectives 18

Persuasive writing skills 19
   Persuasive structure 19
   Pathos, ethos, and logos 19
   Persuasive writing techniques 20
   Persuasive speaking techniques 21
   Preparing for an oral presentation 21

SPELLING, PUNCTUATION, AND GRAMMAR 22

Spelling 22
   Commonly misspelled words 22
   Homophones and mnemonics 22
   How to improve spelling 23

Punctuation 24
   Types and effects 24
   Common punctuation mistakes 24

Grammar 25
   Word classes 25
   Clauses and sentence fragments 26
   Subject and object 26
   Types of sentences 27

Vocabulary 28
   Replacement words 28
   Words to describe tone 28
   High-level vocabulary 29

Miralo Education Group Ltd owner of SnapRevise® trademark, 6 Cranwell Road, Locking Parklands, Weston-super-Mare, BS24 7GF, United Kingdom
Copyright © Miralo Education Group 2026, Published by Miralo Education Group Ltd CN 15550989
All rights reserved. These notes are protected by copyright owned by Miralo Education Group Ltd and you may not reproduce, disseminate, or communicate to the public the whole or a substantial part thereof except as permitted at law or with the prior written consent of Miralo Education Group Ltd.
Title: GCSE English Language Summary Notes
ISBN: 978-1-917424-81-3
Disclaimer: No reliance on warranty. These SnapRevise materials are intended to supplement but are not intended to replace or be any substitute for your regular school attendance, for referring to prescribed texts, or for your own note taking. You are responsible for following the appropriate syllabus, attending school classes, and maintaining good study practices. It is your responsibility to evaluate the accuracy of any information, opinions, and advice in these materials. Under no circumstance will Miralo Education Group Ltd ("Publishers"), their officers, agents, or employees be liable for any loss or damage caused by your use or reliance on these materials, including any adverse impact upon your performance in any academic subject as a result of your use or reliance on the materials. You accept that all information provided or made available by the Publishers is in the nature of general information and does not constitute advice. It is not guaranteed to be error-free and you should always independently verify any information, including through use of a professional teacher and other reliable resources. To the extent permissible at law, the Publishers expressly disclaim all warranties or guarantees of any kind, whether express or implied, including without limitation any warranties concerning the accuracy or content of information provided in these materials or other fitness for purpose. The Publishers shall not be liable for any direct, indirect, special, incidental, consequential or punitive damages of any kind. You agree to indemnify the Publishers, its officers, agents, and employees against any loss whatsoever by using these materials.

Reading skills

Speed reading strategies for comprehension

Below are a range of strategies you can use to approach source texts and extracts in exam conditions. You can test out any combination of these to find ones that best help you efficiently comprehend the material so that you can maximise the time you have to write your answers.

Skimming: quickly scanning the text to get a general understanding of content, key ideas, and structure. This can be accomplished by moving down the page in a zig-zag pattern and limiting yourself to about 30 seconds for a full page of text. The aim is not to understand or remember everything but to get a general impression of the text so that you could answer very basic questions (i.e. does the character feel afraid or excited? Is the weather welcoming or dangerous? etc.)

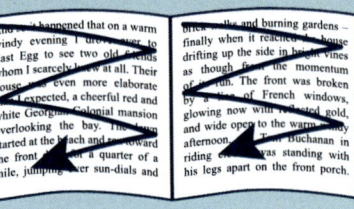

Scanning: a more focused form of reading where you look for specific information such as names, numbers, or key words without needing to read the entire text in detail. This works especially well if you read the key words or phrases in the questions first, then scan the text for those terms.

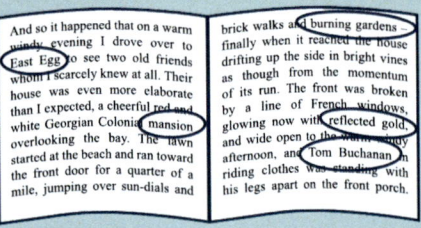

Finger-guided reading: use your finger to guide your eye in speed reading. Move your finger at a smooth but fast pace (e.g. 1 second per line) and don't focus on reading word-for-word – just form a general impression of the passage.

Chunking: break the text up into more manageable sections and just focus on understanding or summarising each one. This is made easier if your source text has paragraph breaks. This can help prevent you from feeling overwhelmed with a long text. It also helps highlight the sequence of information within the text and map out the progression of ideas.

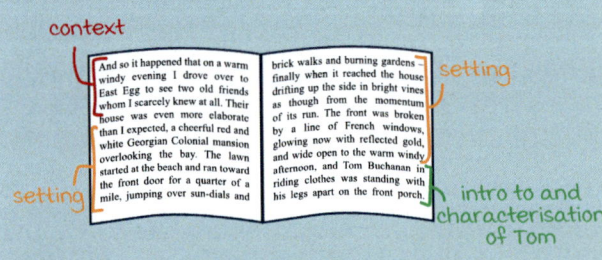

Selective reading: involves only paying attention to specific sections of text while ignoring others or leaving them for a more in-depth reading later. Again, this is helpful with longer texts and can help you eliminate extraneous information. For instance, you could only read the first and last sentence of each paragraph. Furthermore, it encourages you to ignore words you may not know on your first reading so that you can just focus on the core ideas of the text without getting bogged down with individual words.

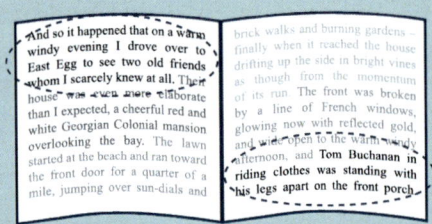

Visualisation: create a mental image of the text as it unfolds. By the end, you will know which elements of the text are important because they will dominate your visualisation. It will also make the information within the text more memorable, thereby helping you answer questions faster. In addition, you'll have an advantage for any questions that ask you to explain something 'in your own words,' as you can draw from your own visualisation as opposed to just relying on quotes from the text.

Reading skills

What to look for in texts

First impressions
- Start with your initial thoughts after having read the text once. Ask yourself 'what do I think, feel, or believe?'
- Brainstorm a list of points or interpretations.
- For each point, ask yourself 'how do I know?' This will prompt you to go back to the text and find evidence to back up your initial thoughts.
- When you write your analysis, just reverse the order of these questions so that you first present evidence from the text and then explain how it supports an idea.
- E.g. The author's use of ridiculous imagery in characterising the "effeminate swank" of Tom's clothing as well as the semantic field of superiority seen in words like "supercilious" and "arrogant" strongly suggest that the narrator dislikes Tom and sees him as a fool worthy of contempt.

Look for meaningful moments
If something stands out in the passage to you, trust your instincts! Maybe it's a specific choice of words, an emotional moment, or a point that is given special emphasis. If it seems important to you as a reader, it probably is, so pay attention to these parts and ask yourself 'why is this important?' or 'what is the author trying to do here?'

Look for structural features
Depending on the type of text, this can include:
- Paragraph order
- Contrasts/juxtaposition
- Tonal shifts
- Shifts in perspective
- Sense of progression from beginning to end
- Flashbacks/non-linear narrative

Read the questions first
- Reading the exam questions before reading the passage is a good way to ensure your mind will be primed for the most relevant information in the passage.
- For example, if question 1 is about the character's appearance, and question 2 is about the character's relationship with their parents, you will naturally pay more attention to any moments in the source text that mention their appearance or parents.
- Likewise, if the text opens with a lengthy description of the setting but none of the questions are about the setting, then you can skim read that part quicker and perhaps revisit it later if you need additional evidence for a 10+ mark extended response.

> And so it happened that on a warm windy evening I drove over to East Egg to see two old friends whom I scarcely knew at all. Their house was even more elaborate than I expected, a cheerful red and white Georgian Colonial mansion overlooking the bay. The lawn started at the beach and ran toward the front door for a quarter of a mile, jumping over sun-dials and brick walks and burning gardens—finally when it reached the house drifting up the side in bright vines as though from the momentum of its run. The front was broken by a line of French windows, glowing now with reflected gold, and wide open to the warm windy afternoon, and Tom Buchanan in riding clothes was standing with his legs apart on the front porch.
>
> He had changed since his New Haven years. Now he was a sturdy, straw haired man of thirty with a rather hard mouth and a supercilious manner. Two shining, arrogant eyes had established dominance over his face and gave him the appearance of always leaning aggressively forward. Not even the effeminate swank of his riding clothes could hide the enormous power of that body—he seemed to fill those glistening boots until he strained the top lacing and you could see a great pack of muscle shifting when his shoulder moved under his thin coat. It was a body capable of enormous leverage—a cruel body.
>
> His speaking voice, a gruff husky tenor, added to the impression of fractiousness he conveyed. There was a touch of paternal contempt in it, even toward people he liked—and there were men at New Haven who had hated his guts.
>
> – Extract from *The Great Gatsby* by F. Scott Fitzgerald

What do I think / feel / believe?	How do I know?
Tom's house is fancy	- Word choice ("elaborate," "cheerful," "mansion") - Polysyndeton ("sun-dials and brick walls and burning gardens" imply endless wealth) - Imagery ("glowing now with reflected gold")
The narrator doesn't like Tom	- Ridiculous imagery ("effeminate swank of his riding clothes [...] standing with his legs apart on the front porch") - Semantic field of superiority ("supercilious," "arrogant," "dominance")
There will be a fight later involving Tom	- Word choice ("cruel body") foreshadows his capacity for selfish violence - Focus on physicality rather than his emotions ("glistening boots" and "great pack of muscle") but no description of his inner world

Look for language features
- Look for obvious techniques like imagery, metaphors, similes, etc.
- Annotate past papers by highlighting every language feature you can find so that this becomes an automatic process.
- In the exam there's no need to highlight everything, but training your brain to naturally pick up on techniques will make it much easier to find evidence to support your answers.

Reading skills

Annotation strategies

Language feature-based approach
- Identify and highlight meaningful techniques.
- Briefly annotate the effect of this language.
- Focus on making connections between language and authorial intent.
- Don't worry about essay structure or how you could connect these ideas – just find as much evidence as you can.
- This is the best approach if you find yourself running out of ideas or unsure of what to analyse.
- Stop annotating when you can't find any more language features, then pick out the strongest examples to write your analysis.

Question-based approach
- Assign one highlighter colour or symbol per exam question.
- Highlight the passage by finding evidence related to each question.
- Focus on finding the most relevant parts of the passage that will best enable you to answer the question.
- Don't worry about identifying techniques – you can do this later if needed after you've found and categorised the evidence.
- This is the best approach if you find your writing lacks structure, if you repeat yourself too often, or if you get 'writer's block' and feel stuck when trying to find evidence in exam conditions.
- This is also great for long texts and for following the progression of themes/ideas/characters across the passage.
- Stop annotating when you think you have enough evidence to satisfy the mark scheme for each question.

Annotations on the left passage:

- **Contradiction, conveys confusion and sense of strangeness** — "warm windy evening"; "two old friends whom I scarcely knew at all"
- **Alliteration, establishes setting**
- **Characterisation of house implies wealth and opulence** — "elaborate"; "cheerful red and white Georgian Colonial mansion overlooking the bay"
- **Polysyndeton to suggest excess** — "sun-dials and brick walks and burning gardens"
- **Vivid imagery connoting radiance and furthering the depiction of wealth** — "glowing now with reflected gold"
- **Kinaesthetic imagery and personification, making the lawn seem alive and drawing the speaker into the house** — "momentum"
- **Compound sentence structure; character is introduced at the end with the whole paragraph building up towards him, heightening tension**

Passage text:

> And so it happened that on a warm windy evening I drove over to East Egg to see two old friends whom I scarcely knew at all. Their house was even more elaborate than I expected, a cheerful red and white Georgian Colonial mansion overlooking the bay. The lawn started at the beach and ran toward the front door for a quarter of a mile, jumping over sun-dials and brick walks and burning gardens—finally when it reached the house drifting up the side in bright vines as though from the momentum of its run. The front was broken by a line of French windows, glowing now with reflected gold, and wide open to the warm windy afternoon, and Tom Buchanan in riding clothes was standing with his legs apart on the front porch.

Question-based annotation example:

0 1	How does the author explore nature as a setting in this extract?	2 marks
0 2	What impression does this passage create of the East Egg house?	3 marks
0 3	How does this passage use imagery to create a sense of movement?	3 marks

Passage text:

> And so it happened that on a warm windy evening I drove over to East Egg to see two old friends whom I scarcely knew at all. Their house was even more elaborate than I expected, a cheerful red and white Georgian Colonial mansion overlooking the bay. The lawn started at the beach and ran toward the front door for a quarter of a mile, jumping over sun-dials and brick walks and burning gardens—finally when it reached the house drifting up the side in bright vines as though from the momentum of its run. The front was broken by a line of French windows, glowing now with reflected gold, and wide open to the warm windy afternoon, and Tom Buchanan in riding clothes was standing with his legs apart on the front porch.

Reading skills

Understanding evidence in texts

Inferring meaning from context

- Outside of exam conditions, it's a good idea to annotate any words you've never seen before or that you don't know the meaning of (so that you can boost your vocabulary!).
- In exam conditions, you could simply ignore these and choose other quotes as evidence, but just to make sure you haven't misunderstood the text, it's good to check these words using the surrounding context now that you have a grasp on the overall ideas and the focus of the questions.
- For example, consider the following lines from the previous extract of *The Great Gatsby*, and suppose you didn't know the meaning of the highlighted words. You could still infer their meaning from the context of the passage, as shown in these 'train of thought' annotations.

> His speaking voice, a gruff husky tenor, added to the impression of fractiousness he conveyed. There was a touch of paternal contempt in it, even toward people he liked—and there were men at New Haven who had hated his guts.

fractiousness: I don't know this word, but based on the passage the author is depicting the character as swaggering and looking for a fight. Maybe it's close to 'fracture' meaning he's about to break, like a hard object.

tenor: I think it has something to do with music? And this sentence is about his voice, so this might be auditory imagery to describe the essence of his voice.

contempt: I don't know this word but the structure of the sentence means I know this is something bad. I could replace this with another word like 'There was a touch of distaste in it, even toward people he liked' – the word 'even' implies that he doesn't just act surly and arrogant around people he doesn't like. I know paternal has something to do with fathers, so maybe this is about him acting superior and treating other people like children, or like he has the right to order them around.

Finding evidence and implications

Inferences are conclusions drawn from information in the text, even if it's not directly stated. You'll need to interpret implicit meaning and read between the lines.

- **Explicit evidence:** things clearly stated in the text (e.g. what clothes is Tom wearing?)
- **Implicit evidence:** things that the text hints at or subtly suggests through the author's choice of words and use of techniques (e.g. what emotions does the narrator feel towards Tom?)

You should also distinguish between the different levels of likely ideas or interpretations.

- **Strong implicature:** something that is heavily implied or very obvious in the text. An example of strong implicature from the passage above would be that Tom is a wealthy and egotistical character as there is lots of explicit and implicit evidence to support this. Therefore, this would be a strong point to make in a body paragraph as we could easily justify this idea and back it up with quotes and techniques.
- **Weak implicature:** something that is an unlikely interpretation based on evidence. An example of weak implicature would be that the narrator has a crush on Tom. You *could* try to argue this based on the narrator's fixation with Tom's body or by cherry-picking examples like his description of Tom's "gruff" voice, but ultimately this isn't clearly supported by the evidence. This interpretation isn't incorrect, but it is weak, so you should opt for something stronger instead.

You can also annotate any combination of the following:

- Key words and phrases
- Language techniques
- Tonal shifts
- Repetition of words or recurring ideas
- Sentence lengths
- Contrasts
- Tone and mood
- Intended effect on the reader
- Writer's purpose

Reading skills

Dissecting questions

Note the question verb as this tells you how much information to give, and in what format (in this case, list = give a simple, plain answer; can be in dot point form).

Always double check which source you need to refer to, and if there are any restrictions on which parts of the source you need to use for this question.

Key concern of this question, telling us what to go back to the passage and look for.

marking scheme can indicate how many answers or how much explanation/analysis is required. In this case, we know we only need to list 3 points, and there are no marks available for explanation or analysis, so don't waste time!

Restriction on answer, meaning we need to find three unique points. Don't repeat yourself or waste time writing any more than what is required. Be precise!

Double check restrictions — now we need to use the entire source, so you should look for a range of examples to form an overall impression

| 0 | 1 | Refer to **lines 1–9** of Source 1. **List 3 aspects** of the **house in East Egg** from this extract.

[3 marks]

1. _____
2. _____
3. _____

Slightly narrows our focus to only structural features, not other language techniques like imagery or alliteration.

| 0 | 2 | How does the author use **structural features** to **organise** the narrator's thoughts in this extract?

Hints that we need to look for evidence to do with the order of information within sentences or paragraphs.

[6 marks]

medium mark allocation means we need to include multiple examples with explanation and analysis

| 0 | 3 | You now need to think about the **whole of the source**. What impression does the writer convey about the character of Tom? You could write about
- How the character of Tom is introduced and positioned
- How the writer uses certain language features to characterise Tom
- How your interpretation of Tom develops over the course of the extract

[10 marks]

List of possible points can guide your answer, though these are not required nor conclusive. Ideally these should be springboards for you to start your answer and then develop more in-depth ideas.

High mark allocation means this is an extended response or mini-essay that requires multiple points, examples, and analytical insights. Allow yourself extra time, and spend at least a minute writing a quick plan to ensure you have a clear argument and logical structure.

Priorities when reading exam questions
- **WHAT** information is being requested?
- **HOW** do you need to answer? Do you need to quote, mention a technique, paraphrase, explain?
- **WHERE** in the text will I find this information?

Analytical writing skills

Word-level close analysis

Treat the marker like an alien!
- Imagine the marker is an alien who has read the text (so you don't need to summarise or explain the plot) but has no understanding of themes, how language conveys meaning, or even basic human emotions.
- Explain everything as if they know nothing. Instead of assuming the marker knows all the right answers, spell it out for them.
- Make your points abundantly clear and specific.
    - E.g. instead of writing:
    'The character changes throughout the text.' ✗
    ... you could instead write:
    'The author presents the character's descent into tyranny through his increasing reliance on violence and suppression of his empathy and humanity.' ✓
    - E.g. analysis like:
    'Lady Macbeth's quote "Out, damned spot" shows that she feels guilty.' ✗
    ... is not specific enough. How do we know this language has this effect? A better version of this would be:
    'Lady Macbeth's desperate repetition of "out" shows her increasing panic as she attempts to erase her guilt. The word "damned" links to religious imagery, suggesting she fears eternal punishment.' ✓
- Keep your writing logical and structured. Using linking words can help achieve this (e.g. 'This suggests that...' 'Therefore, the author implies...').
- Link everything back to the question at the end. Imagine your alien marker has finished reading your analysis and asks themselves 'so what?' It's your job to answer this question by explaining the significance of this evidence and ultimately answering the exam question.

Questions to ask for word-level analysis
- What is the literal meaning or dictionary definition of this word?
- What are the connotations and implied meanings of this word? What emotions, associations, or ideas does this word make me think of?'
    - E.g. blood could connote violence, guilt, effort, family ties, etc.
- How might this word affect what the reader thinks, feels, or believes about things in the text?
- Is this placement of this word significant? Where in the sentence/passage does it appear. Does it stand alone for emphasis? Is it closely associated with other words in the sentence/passage?
- Why would the author use this word instead of a synonym or similar word?
- Does this word/phrase belongs to a certain semantic field (e.g. death, nature, childhood)? Does this word feel like it's in harmony with the rest of the text, or does it change the mood?
- Does the sound or rhythm of the word enhance its meaning?
- Does the sentence structure or syntax enhance the word's meaning?
- How might different audiences respond differently to this word/phrase? Are there ambiguities or contextual differences that could affect readers' interpretations?
- Is this word (or a synonym or antonym) used elsewhere in the text? Does the pattern or meaning of this word evolve?

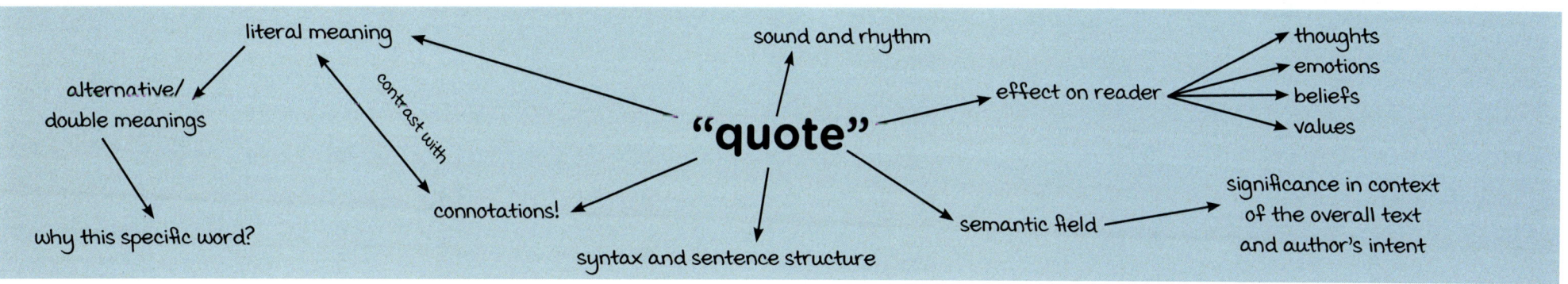

Analytical writing skills

Essay structure

PETAL method
- P: Point
- E: Evidence
- T: Technique
- A: Analysis
- L: Link

P: Point
- Clearly state your idea or argument in response to the question.
- Use key words or synonyms of words from the question to ensure your point is relevant.
- Avoid making vague or generic points – more specificity means more marks!

E: Example
- Choose a specific example from the text to use as evidence.
- Be concise and avoid long excerpts – shorter quotes are better as precise examples.
- Embed the example within your sentence, modifying quotes if necessary.
- Use multiple examples if you need to compare/contrast or build up to a bigger idea.

T: Technique
- Identify the language or structural features used in the quote.
- If there is no formal technique, use metalanguage to comment on the author's choice of words or the overall sense/mood/tone/implications etc.
- Comment on the specific effect of the technique – remember that naming the technique is only step 1! You must be specific about the effect to earn marks

A: Analysis
- Explain how the example creates meaning that supports the author's intent or purpose of the text.
- Consider how the reader is made to think/feel/believe something as a result of the author's choice of words.
- Spend at least one sentence doing a 'deep dive' into how specific language creates a specific effect.
- Never give a general definition or generic effect for a technique. You must always apply your knowledge to the specific example.
- Analysis can consist of: explaining the literal meaning of a quote, discussing why the author has employed a certain technique, demonstrating how certain language contributes to a theme, or considering possible alternate interpretations.

L: Link
- Tie your discussion back to the question or the core message of the text.
- If relevant, refer back to previous ideas to show development or contrast.
- Use linking words to signal that you are 'zooming out' to comment on authorial intent.

Tips
- Not every flower has to have 5 petals! Vary your structure, but make sure you show the marker that you can do all 5.
- Some petal parts will be more effective if combined (e.g. PEETETTAAL, using multiple pieces of evidence, identifying multiple techniques, and then making multiple analysis statements about how these elements work together). Vary your sentences as you get more confident.

Analytical writing skills

Sentence starters for essay writing

P: Point	E: Evidence	T: Technique	A: Analysis	L: Link
The author states/emphasises/explores…	For example, the words…	This use of…	This aids the author in elucidating…	Thus, the author reminds us…
Throughout the text…	The author supports this by…	The ___ here helps to convey…	This reveals that…	This therefore supports the core idea of…
The idea of ___ is shown when…	This is best illustrated by…	By employing ___, the author emphasises…	This effectively positions the reader to believe…	Ultimately, this bolsters the author's claim that…
The key concept presented in this passage is…	One example of this can be seen when…	The author's subtle use of ___ seeks to…	This strengthens the author's message of…	Thus, the author further strengthens their presentation of…
The text explores the notion that…	The author elucidates this when…	This is an instance of ___ - a technique the author uses to…	This implies that…	This can further be seen in…
One of the most salient ideas in this text is…	Perhaps the best example of this is…	Through the repeated use of ___, the author suggests…	This highlights the author's intentions of…	Thus, this section contributes to the author's overall…
This text demonstrates how…	This idea is evidenced by…	The choice of diction in this passage is evocative of…	Through this, the author articulates a broader message of…	Consequently, this implies…
In this section, the author draws attention to…	For instance, the character states…	This symbolism represents…	This reinforces the idea that…	This reinforces the aforementioned…
A recurring idea in this text is…	This is made clear when…	The writer's choice of the word(s) ___ evoke a sense of…	To the reader, this could be interpreted as…	Thus, by drawing attention to ___, the author reveals…
The author's central message of ___ is evident in…	A compelling example of this is…	In particular, the use of ___ contributes to the author's intention by…	The author thereby engenders a sense of…	Therefore, the text suggests…
One of the text's core ideas can be seen when…	The author illustrates this with the quote…	The word ___, with its connotations of ___, emphasise…	This effectively communicates the notion that…	Ultimately then, the author leads us to believe…
The essence of this passage is that…	One palpable example of this is…	Here, the author has used ___ in order to…	The author's decision to foreground ___ is significant because…	This is further developed later in the text by…

Analytical writing skills

Integrating quotes

Rules for grammatically integrating quotes
- Embed quotes naturally into your own sentences.
- Avoid inserting quotes in standalone sentences or without context.
- Use square brackets to modify words for clarity, grammatical consistency, or to adjust the tense.
    - E.g. *Atticus states that he "wanted [Scout] to see what real courage [was], instead of getting the idea that courage [was] a man with a gun in his hand.*
- Use ellipses to omit unnecessary words
    - E.g. *Atticus juxtaposes the idea of "real courage" ... [and] a man with a gun in his hand" to imply that acts of violent and intimidation are products of fear, not bravery.*

Tips for sophisticated quote analysis
- Use short, impactful quotes rather than overloading your sentences with long excerpts.
- If you need to use a longer quote for context, follow it up by zooming in on one or two particular words or phrases and conduct close analysis.
    - E.g. *Lady Macbeth calls on dark spirits to "unsex [her] here, and fill [her] from the crown to the toe top-full of direst cruelty." In particular, the use of the word "unsex" reflects her abject repudiation of her femininity, whilst her choice of the word "crown" to refer to her head hints at her thirst for power and recognition.*
- Blend quotes with analytical verbs (e.g. reveals, highlights, underscores) to show that you are unpacking the meaning of a quote, not merely summarising it.

Levels of quote analysis

Original quote from the text	"I wanted you to see what real courage is, instead of getting the idea that courage is a man with a gun in his hand." - *To Kill A Mockingbird* (spoken by Atticus to his daughter Scout)
Unintegrated quote (avoid!) ✗	*Atticus frequently imparts moral lessons to his children. "I wanted you to see what real courage is." This shows he is a very admirable character.*
Integrated quote (good) ✓	*Atticus tells Scout "I wanted you to see what real courage is," which has a profound impact on her view of the world.*
Blended quote (using square brackets to modify grammar or replace words) (good) ✓	*Atticus reveals that he "wanted [Scout] to see what real courage is" so that she would develop a more nuanced view of the world and not view courage as simply "a man with a gun in his hand."*
Analysed quote (best!) ✓✓	*Atticus' desire for Scout "to see what real courage is" showcases his compassion and foresight as a father, and suggests to readers that he is extremely cautious of the impressions of the world that his children are forming.*

Analytical writing skills

Comparative analysis

Comparative topic sentences
- Similarity:
  - Throughout both Text A and Text B, the idea of _____ has a profound impact on the characters.
  - In Text A and Text B, the authors present us with…
  - Both Author A and Author B challenge the notion that…
  - The concept of _____ is a key concern in both Text A and Text B.
  - Text A and Text B both seek to highlight…
- Difference:
  - Whilst Text A and Text B both explore notions of _____, they do so in slightly different ways.
  - Where Author A suggests that _____, Author B instead condones…
  - Text A's presentation of _____ as _____ is challenged by Text B which instead suggests…
  - Throughout Text A and Text B, readers are exposed to differing perspectives of…
  - In Text A, Author A establishes a sense of _____ that stands in contrast to Author B's depiction of…

Comparative concluding sentences
- Similarity:
  - To this end, both Author A and Author B seek to communicate…
  - Therefore, Text A and Text B are unified in their portrayal of…
  - Thus, both authors share a similar desire for…
  - In spite of the subtle differences in their approach to _____, both Text A and Text B suggest that…
  - Hence, the notion of _____ is of paramount importance to readers' understanding of both Text A and Text B.
- Difference:
  - Thus, whilst both texts are concerned with the notion of _____, ultimately, Author A and Author B present very different ideas about…
  - Therefore, where Text A acts as an indictment of _____, Text B instead contends that…
  - Whilst the idea of _____ is common to both texts, the nature of the authors' messages are distinct in that…
  - Thus, the concept of _____ can be seen to play a vastly different role in both Text A and Text B.
  - Consequently, Author A and Author B both adopt markedly different stances towards the question of…

Types of comparison
- You can make connections in the form of **similarities** and differences in either the **textual features** or **meaning** of a text.
- These combinations give us **4 types** of comparison, and you should aim to showcase all 4 in your writing.

  1. **Similarities in textual features**
     e.g. both authors use the motif of blood to symbolise guilt
  2. **Similarities in meaning/intent**
     e.g. both authors convey the horrors of war and its destruction of innocence
  3. **Differences in textual features**
     e.g. where Author A uses subtle connotations, Author B is instead more overt and uses hyperbole
  4. **Differences in meaning/intent**
     e.g. where Author A focuses on the victims of war, Author B by contrast focuses blame on the powerful

11

Analytical writing skills

Foundational techniques

The definitions and effects/intentions in the tables here are included to help you understand the techniques, but you should never write these explanations in your answers or essays. You need to be specific when commenting on the effect, so general explanations like this won't earn you any marks!

Technique	Definition	Example	Effect/intention
Symbolism	Using objects or things to represent abstract ideas or qualities	"Blood will have blood" - Macbeth	Uses simple, tangible things as a focus in order to convey deeper meanings about big, abstract themes and messages
Metaphor	A figure of speech that describes one thing as another	"Juliet is the sun!" - Romeo and Juliet	Create comparisons that make emotions and ideas more intense
Simile	A figure of speech that use 'like' or 'as' to describe something	"as gentle as a lamb" - Romeo and Juliet	Explicitly links or compares two things to create a strong association between them
Repetition	Repeating words, phrases, sounds, or structures	"Sleep no more! Macbeth does murder sleep', the innocent sleep, Sleep that knits up..." - Macbeth	Strengthens emphasis, reinforces core ideas, builds rhythm, or contributes to a sense of urgency or persuasion
Imagery	Appeals to the senses and creates a vivid image in the reader's mind	"Marley's face. It was not in impenetrable shadow as the other subjects in the yard were, but had a dismal light about it, like a bad lobster in a dark cellar." - A Christmas Carol	Immerses the reader an enhances the atmosphere of the text by making them imagine what they could see/hear/smell/taste/touch/feel
Listing	Includes multiple elements of something in quick succession	"The cold within him froze his old features, nipped his pointed nose, shriveled his cheek, stiffened his gait; made his eyes red, his thin lips blue..." - A Christmas Carol	Builds intensity or conveys a sense of abundance, magnitude, and scale
Hyperbole	Exaggeration used for emphasis	"every idiot who goes about with 'Merry Christmas,' on his lips, should be boiled with his own pudding" - A Christmas Carol	Conveys a sense of extremity and magnifies the importance, urgency, desperation, or enormity of something
Euphemism	An expression to avoid directly saying something distasteful, unpleasant, or confronting	"As if a girl of that sort would refuse money." - An Inspector Calls	Softens harsh or uncomfortable truths, creating a more palatable or indirect tone that can either obscure reality or hint at something more delicately or sensitively.
Colloquial language	Informal or conversational words and phrases	"You ain't got good sense. It's too soon.' 'It ain't too soon. If it was ah year from now it would be too soon." - Their Eyes Were Watching God	Adds authenticity and relatability to a text, shaping character voice and grounding the writing in a specific cultural or social context.

Analytical writing skills

Connotations	Implied or suggested meanings of a word beyond its literal definition	Romeo calls Juliet a "holy shrine" which has religious connotations to emphasise his reverence for her.	Shapes tone and mood, subtly influencing how readers perceive a subject, and evokes specific associations that a simpler word might not.
Irony	A contrast between expectation and reality	"My name is Ozymandias, King of Kings; Look on my Works, ye Mighty, and despair!" – Ozymandias	Can create humour, suspense, or hint at a deeper truth by encouraging the audience to think critically
Alliteration	The repetition of certain sounds or letter combinations	"rifles' rapid rattle" – Anthem for Doomed Youth	Can create rhythm and enhance flow, or strengthen the association between the words or ideas that are related through alliteration
Personification	Giving human characteristics to objects or abstract concepts	The Ghost of Christmas Past is a personification of memory in A Christmas Carol	Fosters an emotional and human connection to ideas that might otherwise be hard to relate to
Juxtaposition	Deliberately placing two things together to draw attention to their differences	"Present fears are less than horrible imaginings" – Macbeth	Highlights differences and emphasises the discrepancy between two things that might not be obvious if we just viewed one thing in isolation
Allusion	Referencing another text, historical event, or idea	"Will all great Neptune's ocean wash this blood clean from my hand?" (allusion to Roman god) – Macbeth	Adds to the meaning of the text by inviting readers to draw connections based on their own historical, literary, or cultural experiences and understanding
Oxymoron	A figure of speech that combines two contradictory words	"He's a beautiful tyrant! A fiendish angel!" – Romeo and Juliet	Creates a striking contrast that can emphasise complexity, irony, or paradox
Caesura	A pause within a line of verse (e.g. when a poem contains a full stop and the start of a new sentence within the same line) – this is the opposite of enjambment	"Nothing beside remains. Round the decay" – Ozymandias	Introduces a deliberate pause within a line, affecting rhythm and pacing while emphasising key ideas or emotional shifts. Often it draws our attention to the word just before the caesura (e.g. "remains") and makes us pause there while the meaning of that word sinks in.
Enjambment	When one line of poetry continues into the next without a break at the end – this is the opposite of a caesura	"Two vast and trunkless legs of stone / Stand in the desert" – Ozymandias	Propels the reader forward by breaking a phrase or sentence across multiple lines, generating suspense, fluidity, interconnectedness, or a sense of urgency.
Onomatopoeia	Where the sound of the word itself imitates the sound being described (e.g. buzz, ring, pitter-patter)	"It shushes. / It hushes / The loudness in the road. / It flitter-twitters" – Cynthia in the Snow	Immerses the reader by mimicking real sounds, enhancing vividness and sensory engagement in descriptions.

Analytical writing skills

Advanced techniques

These are some less common techniques that most students won't know about. However, mentioning these doesn't guarantee you'll get a high mark. The most important thing is that you provide **analysis of specific words** rather than name-dropping fancy techniques. So refer to this list to expand the range of techniques available to you, but always focus on analysing the specific effect!

Technique		Definition	Example	Effect/intention
Metonymy		A figure of speech where an object or symbol is used to represent something bigger (e.g. 'the crown' to mean the monarchy)	"The hand that mocked them, and the heart that fed" - *Ozymandias*	Creates concise, symbolic connections between concepts, making language more vivid and engaging. It helps reinforce themes by linking abstract ideas to concrete images.
Asyndeton		Omission of conjunctions in a list (i.e. not having 'and' before the last item in a list)	"I came, I saw, I conquered." - *Julius Caesar*	Speeds up the rhythm of a sentence, creating urgency, intensity, excitement, chaos, or a sense of endlessness.
Polysyndeton		Excessive use of conjunctions in a list (i.e. using 'and' or 'or' in between every item in a list)	"If there be cords, or knives, Poison, or fire, or suffocating streams, I'll not endure it." - *Othello*	Slows down the pace of a sentence, making it more dramatic and weighty to emphasise abundance, overwhelming emotion, or breathlessness.
Pathetic fallacy		Human emotions attributed to nature or inanimate objects, often reflecting inner feelings in the external world (e.g. in the weather or setting)	"The night has been unruly" - *Macbeth*	Reflects characters' emotions through their surroundings, enhancing mood and atmosphere, or strengthening links between nature and humanity.
Synaesthesia		Describing one kind of sense using another (e.g. yellow music, a warm smile)	"In some melodious plot of beechen green" - *Ode to a Nightingale*	Creates rich imagery that blurs the boundaries between senses, making descriptions more vivid and imaginative.
Types of imagery	**Visual:** descriptive language that appeals to the sense of sight		"The yellow fog that rubs its back upon the window panes" - *The Lovesong of J. Alfred Prufrock*	Helps readers picture scenes, settings, and characters more vividly, making it easier to convey complex ideas (since a picture is worth a thousand words!).
	Auditory: descriptive language that appeals to the sense of sound		"suddenly there came a tapping, as of someone gently rapping, rapping at my chamber door." - *The Raven*	Makes scenes more immersive by engaging the reader's sense of hearing. This can enhance realism or heighten the atmosphere.
	Gustatory: descriptive language that appeals to the sense of taste		"The chocolate river was rich and creamy, flowing like a dream come true." - *Charlie and the Chocolate Factory*	Can convey pleasure, disgust, or evoke strong sensory experiences. This makes descriptions of food or taste-related moments more vivid.
	Olfactory: descriptive language that appeals to the sense of smell		"the river warehouses with their faint redolences of bananas and coffee." - *A Streetcar Named Desire*	Immerses the reader in a setting, triggering memories or emotions associated with scent. This can create a powerful atmosphere or contrast between pleasant and unpleasant experiences, deepening our sensory engagement with the narrative.
	Tactile/kinaesthetic: descriptive language that conveys movement or physical sensation		"And so we beat on, boats against the current, borne back ceaselessly into the past." - *The Great Gatsby*	Makes actions and sensations feel real and dynamic. It enhances tension, excitement, or discomfort, depending on the context, and can help readers physically relate to characters' experiences.

Analytical writing skills

Types of alliteration	**Plosives:** repetition of harsh, explosive consonant sounds like p, b, t, d, k, g.	"His terror's touchy dynamite." - *Bayonet Charge*	Creates a forceful, abrupt, or aggressive tone. It can emphasise intensity, drama, disgust, or conflict.
	Fricatives: repetition of soft, airy sounds like f, v, th.	"find them, find them, Round the corner. Through the first gate, / Into our first world, shall we follow / The deception of the thrush?" - *Burnt Norton*	Create a sense of smoothness, whisper-like quality, or even menace. It can evoke a dreamy, soothing, or sinister tone depending on the context.
	Sibilance: repetition of soft, hissing sounds like s, z, sh.	"no stacks or stooks that can be lost" - *Storm on the Island*	Creates a hissing, eerie, or hypnotic effect. It can add suspense, sensuality, or secrecy to a passage.
Euphony	'Nice' sounding words and phrases	"Season of mists and mellow fruitfulness" - *To Autumn*	Enhances the musicality of language through harmonious sounds, evoking a sense of calm, beauty, or fluidity in poetry and prose.
Cacophony	Unpleasant sounding words or phrases	"With throats unslaked, with black lips baked" - *The Rime of the Ancient Mariner*	Disrupts the flow of language with harsh, discordant sounds, creating tension, unease, or emphasis on chaotic or jarring moments.
Types of irony	**Verbal irony:** saying the opposite of what is meant, often with a sarcastic tone.	"And Brutus is an honourable man" - Mark Antony in *Julius Caesar*, (when he's actually sarcastically criticising Brutus for betraying Caesar)	Can add humour or provide subtle criticism of a character or situation.
	Situational irony: when an outcome is the opposite of what is expected.	"A pair of star-crossed lovers take their life" - *Romeo and Juliet*	Heightens the emotional impact by subverting our expectations and contrasting hopes or first impressions with reality.
	Dramatic irony: when the audience knows something that the characters do not	"None of woman born shall harm Macbeth." - *Macbeth*	Engages the audience and amplifies a sense of anticipation or dread, building tension as a narrative approaches something tragic and inevitable.
Antithesis	Two contrasting statements with a similar structure or rhythm (can also refer to polar opposites, e.g. Voldemort is the antithesis of kindness)	"It was the best of times, it was the worst of times" - *A Tale of Two Cities*	Creates stark contrast and emphasises opposing ideas.
Appositives	A noun or noun phrase placed next to another noun to clarify or add detail, often as a parenthetical phrase (surrounded by commas or dashes).	"She was dressed in rich materials—satins, and lace and silks—all of white." - *Great Expectations*	provide additional information efficiently, reducing redundancy. They clarify relationships between ideas and enhance descriptive writing. They can also create a formal or literary tone when used skillfully.
Epithets	An adjective or phrase used to express a characteristic of a character	"Great Gatsby" attributes the epithet of 'great' to aggrandise him	Enhance descriptions by attaching characteristic traits to people, places, or things, reinforcing key themes through association.

Imaginative writing skills

Key strategies

What to do	How to do it
Understand the prompt	• Identify the core idea or emotion that you will use as the basis for your writing. • For worded prompts, spend some time thinking about less obvious ideas and implications or alternate meanings. • For visual prompts, look for more subtle background details that you can also weave into your stories.
Write an effective opening that immediately hooks the reader	• Use an intriguing or unexpected opening line (e.g. a question, line of dialogue, or mysterious remark). • Start in medias res (in the middle of the action) for instant engagement. • Open by describing something that is deeply symbolic to set the tone for your piece. • Introduce the setting subtly, using sensory details or techniques like imagery. • Make us intrigued about the main character by showing us their personality or making us want to know more about them.
Be deliberate in your choice of structure	• No matter what form you choose, you need to include some elements of a beginning/orientation (where you introduce the who/what/when/where/why), a middle/complication (where you build up the atmosphere and give us the main focus or challenge to be overcome), and an ending/resolution (where you tie up loose ends and leave us with your overall message). • If you deviate from this conventional story structure, make sure you have a good reason (e.g. if you are leaving your story unresolved to represent how sometimes there are no easy answers to complex problems).
Plan your piece so that you can develop your structure	• Use a five-sentence plot plan: 1. Introduce your main character(s) and/or setting, 2. Hint at the main conflict or theme, 3. Develop the tension or mood, 4. Create a climax, turning point, or moment of realisation, and 5. Resolve the conflict and leave us with a powerful ending, such as a profound question, final thought, or bookend that calls back to the start of your piece. • Avoid abrupt endings (or running out of time!) by planning your ending in advance and making sure you leave at least a few minutes to write it. • Avoid overcomplicated plots or poor pacing by keeping your narrative simple.
Establish atmosphere and build tension	• Use all 5 senses throughout your piece to immerse the reader, and 'show, don't tell' (see the next section) to describe thoughts and feelings. • Use figurative language techniques such as similes, metaphors, personification, pathetic fallacy, and alliteration to create your desired atmosphere. • Vary your sentence structure (e.g. short sentences for tension or blunt truths; long sentences for flowing descriptions and stream-of-consciousness). • Use contrast and juxtaposition to strengthen one idea by comparing it to another.
Use characterisation to make the people in your narratives feel real	• Show personality through actions, thoughts, and dialogue. You can also use unique speech patterns or small quirks to make characters memorable. • Give your characters clear motivations: what do they want and why? What are they afraid of? What do they hope for the future? Even if you don't explicitly write these things into your story, you should still be able to answer these questions yourself to ensure your characters are well-rounded. • Use inner monologues to achieve greater character depth. Try to capture their voice authentically by choosing words and phrases that would make sense for your character.
Use a consistent, and meaningful narrative perspective	• Choose between first person, second person, and third person point of view. First person is easy to write, creates intimacy and allows for emotional insights. Second person is generally not recommended as this is quite challenging and unconventional, but can immerse the reader. Third person allows for multiple viewpoints and intrigue, though can be harder to manage and might confuse the reader if not done clearly. • Use a consistent tense (if in doubt, past tense is easiest).
Convey your writing style and show off your abilities	• Vary your sentence structures to avoid repetition and enhance atmosphere. • Use punctuation for effect (e.g. ellipses for suspense, dashes for interruptions or emphasis). • Use precise vocabulary that is appropriate for your setting, voice, mood, and intent. • Employ a range of language techniques (see pages 12–15).

Imaginative writing skills

Show, don't tell

You should always aim to *show* things to your reader and not merely *tell* them how things are, revealing and hint at ideas, emotions, or beliefs, rather than explicitly stating them in a boring, factual way. For example, compare the following samples.

> When Jules woke up that morning, he knew it was going to be a bad day. The weather was awful and he was dreading the presentation he'd have to give at work in front of his bosses. They were definitely going to hate his ideas, even though he'd spent all week trying to improve them. But he just wasn't any good at coming up with marketing strategies. It wasn't his fault... he'd just stumbled into this job with a bit of blind luck, and now it was too late for him to ask for help. He wished his girlfriend Amanda were still with him – she could always say the right thing and make him feel better. He got out of bed and got dressed with a pit of dread in his stomach that he knew would be there all day until it was eventually replaced with a feeling of failure after the presentation.

This sample *tells* us about this character and his predicament, but as readers, we are just being fed information, and none of it lets us visualise or empathise with this story. Now let's look at another sample.

> Jules was awoken by streaks of dusty sunlight sneaking through his cheap plastic blinds. His first glimpse of the day was of his stained bedroom floor, strewn with pages of his messy handwriting (almost all of it crossing out) and boxes from last night's Chinese take out comfort food. He let out a prolonged grumble, too sleep-deprived to stop the grumble once it started, and covered his face with a pillow. Perhaps, he thought, if I don't rock up, they'll think I've died! I'll let my phone ring out when the office calls, and everyone will think I've been hit by a car or had an aneurysm or something. That'd be sick.
>
> But it seemed he'd at least had one good idea yesterday – setting his phone alarm volume to max and putting it on the other side of the room, forcing him to heave out of bed minutes later to silence its aggressive blaring. Too late to have a shower and too queasy for his normal greasy bacon breakfast, he pulled open his wardrobe to find his least ill-fitting shirt and pants. His bleary eyes drifted to the expensive tie rack his girlfriend had bought him when he got the job two years ago, even though he only owned three ties. Since then, he'd managed to lose one of them, along with the girlfriend ('did she steal it?' he wondered, bitterly and baselessly) and so he had an easy choice to make this morning: the grey tie, or the mostly-grey-but-with-blue-and-black-lines tie. He went with the colourful choice. Maybe that would make his day better.

This excerpt is way more engrossing! We actually have some idea of what this character and his surroundings are like. But that's not because the author has told us things directly. Rather, we've been given an assortment of details that show us things, all of which combined to form a portrait of the character.

Detail	What it shows
"dusty sunlight," "cheap plastic blinds" and "stained bedroom floor"	This creates a sense of a squalid, unkempt environment; thus we can infer Jules doesn't keep his room clean, nor does anyone in his life keep it clean for him.
"messy handwriting (almost all of it crossing out)"	Jules is working on something but is frustrated, or making little progress, and he has very little to show for it.
"last night's Chinese take out comfort food"	Jules tried in vain to cheer himself up last night.
"Too late to have a shower and too queasy for his normal greasy bacon breakfast"	This morning is not setting Jules up for success. He doesn't have enough time to get ready or look presentable, and this doesn't seem to be a priority for him given the state of his room.
"he pulled open his wardrobe to find his least ill-fitting shirt and pants"	This implies that all of Jules' clothes are ill-fitting, and that the best thing he can aspire to is finding the least bad ones.
"'did she steal it?' he wondered, bitterly and baselessly"	This was likely a bad break up where Jules was dumped and he still harbours feelings of resentment, even though they are "baseless" and futile (i.e. your girlfriend definitely didn't steal your tie, you idiot).
"the grey tie, or the mostly-grey-but-with-blue-and-black-lines tie"	There is not a lot of variation or excitement in Jules' life. His "colourful" option is still very drab and plain, and he has done nothing in at least two years to expand his range.

Imaginative writing skills

Sensory descriptions

- Sight 👀
  - Focus on colour, light, and movement to create vivid imagery (e.g. 'golden sunlight dripped through the cracks in the blinds').
  - Picture the scene in your mind before trying to write it.
- Sound 🔊
  - Use onomatopoeia (e.g. 'the floorboards creaked and groaned').
  - Find creative ways to describe the absence of sound too (e.g. 'the silence pulsed like a quickening heartbeat').
- Smell 👃
  - Link smells to memory or emotion for a deeper effect (e.g. 'the sharp tang of fresh Spanish oranges from her childhood summers').
  - Use layered smells or unconventional descriptions to add depth (e.g. 'the salty breeze carried hints of fish and regret').
- Taste 👅
  - Describe textures and sensations as well as flavor (e.g. 'the chocolate melted smoothly on her tongue, rich and velvety').
  - Describe non-taste sensations as taste (e.g. 'she swallowed her resentment, fighting the urge to gag at the bitter taste of surrender').
- Touch 🫳
  - Include temperature, texture, and pressure (e.g., 'the sand was hot and rough like pork crackling beneath her feet').
  - Describe how something feels emotionally as well as physically (e.g. 'her soft woolen blanket enveloped her like the hug of a lost loved one').

Avoiding clichés

- Avoid clichés like 'as quiet as a mouse' or 'as fast as lightning' because they're missed opportunities to do something more impressive!
- Create a unique metaphors. by comparing things in unexpected ways rather than using the most obvious comparisons that come to mind.
- Develop authentic dialogue and make conversations sound natural, avoiding overly dramatic or robotic speech.
- Be specific – replace vague descriptions like "a beautiful sunset" with detailed imagery (e.g. 'the sky bled into streaks of amber and crimson').
- Experiment with perspective and structure. Try an unusual viewpoint or non-linear storytelling to add originality.

Point of view (POV) perspectives

- **First person:** (I, me, my, we, our) shares the inner thoughts and experiences of one person. This can give greater insight into that one person's emotional experiences, but it can also be limited by bias and subjectivity as this person may not have a complete understanding of the world and other people's perspectives.
  - E.g. *The Hunger Games* is written in first person POV. This means the author can give us a clear sense of the protagonist Katniss' thoughts and feelings about the word through her eyes, but we don't have access to any information that she doesn't know.
- **Second person:** (you, your) targets the reader directly which can be especially effective in persuasive pieces. This is more unusual for imaginative short stories and makes more sense in other genres like letter writing, opinion articles, or speeches, though you can use it if you have a good reason.
  - E.g. *The Reluctant Fundamentalist* has passages written in second person, addressing us as an unknown character to heighten the novel's tension and unease as it explores themes like cultural alienation and judging people without truly knowing them.
- **Third person:** (he, she, they)
  - **Third person limited:** follows just one character (or one character at a time) so is still somewhat restricted like first person narration as it is only focusing on one person's perspective and experiences.
    * E.g. *A Christmas Carol* is written in third person limited perspective of Scrooge, but also gives the readers insights about the world outside of Scrooge so that we can more accurately judge his character and form conclusions about his flaws.
  - **Third person omniscient:** is where the author/narrator knows every character's thoughts and feelings so can move between them as needed. This gives us unlimited insights into everyone though it can be hard to balance whilst still making each character seem authentic and unique. You can think of this as sounding like an all-knowing god who can see inside the heads of every character and who has assembled all of their perspectives to write a single story.
    * For example, *Pride and Prejudice* is written in third person omniscient style as Jane Austen 'head hops' between characters even within the same sentences whenever it's necessary to explain each character's intentions, or to highlight discrepancies between what different characters think or feel (or to be snarky about characters and create dramatic irony by pointing out things they don't know!).

Persuasive writing skills

Persuasive structure

What to do	How to do it
Clear sequence of ideas	• Write dot point plans to make sure your ideas flow logically. You can start by focusing on the problem then move on to the solution. • Take your audience on a journey e.g. 'here's what's going on' → 'here's why you should care' → 'here's what you should do about it.'
Easy to follow	• Signpost your arguments (e.g. '<u>Firstly</u>, I'm going to explain how we got into this mess. <u>Secondly</u>, I'm going to prove to you who's responsible. And <u>finally</u>, I'm going to tell you how we can fix it.' • Refer forward or back to other arguments (e.g. 'as I have already established' or 'as I will explain later'). • Use linking words like 'furthermore,' 'by contrast,' 'therefore' etc. at the start of sentences to show the link between one idea and the next.
Show causality	• Write 'cause and effect' statements that link an action with an outcome in order to make the audience understand it as good or bad. E.g. 'if we support X, we will be rewarded with Y!' or 'if we allow X to happen, no doubt further disasters like Z will follow!' • Use linking words like 'thus,' 'as a result,' 'consequently' etc. to demonstrate how one thing affects another. • Use techniques like listing, asyndeton, and anaphora to show a chain of causation (e.g. 'Time and time again, we expect better, demand better, deserve better. But time and time again, we are let down.')
Persuade, don't inform	• Add emphatic adjectives and adverbs to convey the emotion you want to evoke in readers (e.g. if you want them to feel outraged, don't just say 'this is a breach of privacy' – say 'this is a disgusting breach of privacy and a callous disregard for human rights'). • Avoid using 'I think' or 'in my opinion' to make arguments stronger and more direct. • Use the same emotions you want the audience to feel (e.g. if you want them to be frustrated, sympathetic, or hopeful, you should sound frustrated, sympathetic, or hopeful too).
Engage the audience	• Open with a hook (e.g. a single word, a short phrase, an unexpected sentence) to capture attention • Make the topic more relevant or personal for your audience (e.g. through an anecdote).
End with inspiration!	• No matter your topic, the end of your speech should aim to motivate the audience to support your argument. • Use a call to action and imperative statements.

Pathos, ethos, and logos

There are three main ways you can target your audience in order to persuade them. The first is **pathos**, which covers appeals to passion and emotion. The second is **ethos**, which is about ethics and credibility. The third is **logos**, which is to do with logic and rationality.

To use **pathos**, you need to appeal to the audience's feelings. Try to elicit sympathy, galvanise anger, or provide inspiration, depending on what best suits your issue. An easy way to do this while delivering your speech is to pretend you are feeling these emotions while reading out your own words.

To use **ethos**, you need to establish some sense of justice or injustice. No one likes it when things are unfair, so if there is some kind of unfairness or inequality involved in your issue, point that out and make your audience understand how awful it is. This works well when you are introducing a problem and then persuading your audience that your proposed solution will address this problem.

To use **logos**, you need to lay things out logically and take your audience through a step-by-step train of thought. This is particularly effective when it creates a 'snowballing' effect (i.e. you start with one idea, and then add more and more arguments like a snowball rolling down a hill getting bigger and bigger, until you end with an overwhelming conclusion that seems undeniable because of how logically you've explained it!).

Persuasive writing skills

Persuasive writing techniques

Persuasive writing is not just about cramming in a bunch of rhetorical questions and emphatic language. You have to consider how to shift the mindset of your audience by appealing to their hearts and minds. It's important that you align yourself with your audience (i.e. don't isolate or attack them) and include fair but effective rebuttals of opposing viewpoints (i.e. without creating 'strawman' arguments, or undermining the strength of your contention). The best persuasive writing will use a combination of logical and emotional appeals, including a range of the following techniques.

Technique	Definition	Example
Hyperbole	Exaggeration or extreme language	'This is the pinnacle of human achievement!'
Rhetorical questions	Asking a question that has an obvious, unspoken answer	'Would you want your family to starve to death?'
Hypophora	Asking and then immediately answering a question	'How can we fix this? By rolling up our sleeves and just doing it!'
High modality	Describes words that convey absolute certainty and definitiveness	E.g. must, always, will, everyone, has to, never
Direct address / pronouns	Using first-person (I/me/my) or second-person (you) pronouns to refer to the speaker and audience	'I know you can all make a difference if you join me in raising awareness.'
Inclusive language	Using collective pronouns (we/us/our) to align yourself with the audience	'If we stand up for ourselves, they cannot take away our rights.'
'Us vs. them' dichotomy	Splits a group in two, usually a good group aligned with the speaker/audience and a bad group that can be attacked or demonised	'We all believe in equality, but those who don't are undermining the fabric of our civil society.'
Prolepsis	Pre-emptively dismantling an opposing argument	'Some may say that this proposal is too extreme, but those people don't understand how dire circumstances are!'
Imperative language	Words or phrases that give commands or urgent, authoritative instructions	'Don't delay! Get up and go support the strike today!'
Comparative language	Words that end in '-er' or proceed 'more ___' that compare one thing to another	'Harder, better, faster, stronger'
Superlative language	Words that end in '-est' or proceed 'most ___' that are the extreme end of a spectrum	'Hardest, best, fastest, strongest'
Tricolon	A group of three words/phrases with a similar structure or rhythm (because things sound satisfying in groups of three)	'We must be brave, just, and true.'
Bookending	Beginning and ending your speech with the same (or similar) phrase or imagery to give your piece a satisfying conclusion	'My mother always said there's no such thing as bad weather, only bad clothing… … So maybe my mother was right to tell me there's no such thing as bad weather, so long as we're prepared for it.'

Persuasive writing skills

Persuasive speaking techniques

Technique	Definition
Power pauses	Deliberately leaving a moment of silence for your words to sink in
Hand gestures	Punctuating your speech with relevant movements to mirror your meaning (e.g. 'on one hand… on the other hand') or to emphasise certain words (e.g. this is the ONLY way *throw your hands out in front in desperation*)
Shift in tempo (faster)	Implies build-up, tension, enormity, or chaos as your voice gets faster and faster
Shift in tempo (slower)	Draws the audience's attention to key words and phrases
Tone	The emotions that are expressed by your voice, often most effective as a tonal shift (e.g. sounding angry when describing a problem, but hopeful when you introduce a solution)

Preparing for an oral presentation

1. Read the draft of your speech aloud while timing yourself. This will help you work out whether you're within the time limits. Do this a couple of times just in case, and remember that you'll probably speak faster on the day, so it's better to be closer to the maximum time limit than the minimum.
2. Find places in your speech where you can do the following:
   - Look up and address the audience directly
   - Slow down your words for dramatic effect
   - Use hand gestures to punctuate what you are saying
   - Make eye contact with the audience
   - Change your tone of voice (e.g. get angrier, softer, more optimistic)
   - Use a 'power pause' (i.e. stay silent for a few seconds after you've made a really powerful point)
   - Make your voice louder (but not too loud – just enough to emphasise something)
   - Change your facial expression or body language
   - Use a prop or visual aid (only if your teacher allows it)
3. Transfer your speech onto cue cards or 'palm cards' that fit into the palm of your hands. If you are a very confident public speaker, or if you want to memorise your speech, you can just transfer bullet point reminders rather than the whole speech word-for-word. However, if you're a nervous speaker or worried you might forget something, you can write it all out!
4. Annotate your cue cards with reminders to yourself to "slow down", "look up", or "use an angry tone" so that you make sure to incorporate this into your delivery.
5. Practise reading your cue cards aloud, time yourself, and check for any extra opportunities to add things from the list above.
6. Get a friend or family member to listen to you practise your speech and have them give you feedback. They don't have to have the expertise or specialist knowledge of an English teacher – just ask them if they've understood your ideas, or if you spoke at the right pace and volume.

Spelling

Commonly misspelled words

- Acceptable
- Achieve
- Acknowledgement
- A lot
- Apparently
- Argument
- Beginning
- Believe
- Completely
- Conscience
- Definitely
- Dependent
- Dilemma
- Disappear
- Embarrass
- Exaggerate
- Existence
- Finally
- Foreign
- Gauge
- Grateful
- Government
- Happened
- Immediately
- Inevitably
- Interrupt
- Occasionally
- Occurrence
- Offering
- Naïve
- Necessary
- Negligible
- Noticeably
- Permanent
- Precise
- Probably
- Receive
- Rhythm
- Separate
- Subconsciously
- Surprise
- Unfortunately

Homophones and mnemonics

- **There / Their / They're**
(there contains 'here' because it's about a place; their has 'heir' because it's about possession; they're = they are)
- **Where / Were / Wear**
(where contains 'here' because it's about a place; wear contains an 'a' because it's about apparel, and were is past tense)
- **Past / Passed**
(past is the noun – e.g. in the past; passed is the verb – e.g. time passed slowly)
- **Whether / Weather**
(I'll check whether the weather is nice)
- **Aloud / Allowed**
(aloud = using your voice loudly, allowed = giving permission or a warrant to do something)
- **To / Too / Two**
(to indicates direction, too = also, two = 2. Remember that 'two' with a 'w' (double-u) is double the number one, whereas 'too' has too many 'o's!)
- **Who's / Whose**
(who's = who is at the door; whose = whose coat is on the door)
- **Which / Witch**
(which = question word, witch = magic creature on a broomstick → can you remember which witch is which? Hint: witches always have toads!)
- **Affect / Effect**
(affect is the verb; effect is the noun)
- **Complement / Compliment**
(two colours complement each other; I'll give you a compliment if I'm nice)
- **Sight / Site**
(sight = seeing something through your glasses, site = a place)
- **Through / Threw**
(through = going from one side to another; threw = past tense of 'throw' e.g. he threw a ball through a window)
- **Break / Brake**
(break = damaging something, brake = stopping something)
- **Waist / Waste**
(waist = part of the body, waste = garbage to be discarded – remember the letter 'i' has a thin waistline!)

Spelling

How to improve spelling

- **Read widely!** Exposure to correct spelling helps reinforce words in your memory and expands your vocabulary.
- **Keep a spelling journal:** write a list of difficult words you have misspelled in the past and review them often. This is most effective if it's handwritten and in a place you see often (e.g. pin it up on your bedroom wall or bathroom mirror).
- **Create flashcards:** using online apps is a great way to enhance memorisation using spaced repetition and testing yourself a few times each week.
- **Build muscle memory**: go through your word lists and handwrite the words so that you acquire the muscle memory of the correct spelling.
- **Watch out for 'Americanized' words:** always use British spelling (e.g. 'colour' not 'color,' and 'realise' not 'realize').
- **Use mnemonics:** start with the list provided here and customise it with your own words and mnemonics.
- **Break words into syllables:** it can sometimes help to break up longer words into syllable units (e.g. *for – tune - ate*).
- **Sound it out:** familiarise yourself with sounding out longer words (e.g. *def - i – nite – ly*) to remember the correct spelling.
- **Get feedback:** hand in essays or practice exams to be marked by a teacher or peer, and take note of any misspellings to add to your list/journal.
- **In exam conditions, save time for proofreading:** if you want to check for spelling specifically, scan through each line backwards so that you can focus on individual words rather than sentence grammar and flow.
- **Learn some etymology:** many English words have Latin or Greek roots (e.g. *pre-* means 'before,' *-ology* means 'the study of.' Identifying prefixes, roots, and suffixes can help you identify common ones, thereby helping your spelling and (bonus!) also helping you identify unfamiliar words.

Greek roots	Meaning	Examples in English
a	opposite of	anomaly, amoral, atypical
anti	against	antithesis, anticlimax, antiwar
anthro	human	anthropology, philanthropy, anthropocene
auto	self	automatic, autobiography, autograph
bio	life	biography, biology, biosphere
chrome	colour	monochromatic, trichrome, polychrome
chrono	time	chronic, synchronise, anachronistic
dyna	power	dynamic, dynasty, dynamite
geo	earth	geography, geology, geode
hyper	over/above	hyperbolic, hyperactive, hyperbola
hypo	under/below	hypothermia, hypothetical, hypodermic
logos	word/study	logic, psychology, analogy
path	feeling	sympathy, apathy, psychopath
pseudo	false	pseudoscience, pseudonym, pseudocode
syn	together	synthesis, syncopate, syntax
tech	skill	technique, technology, technician
tele	from far away	television, telephone, telepathy

Latin roots	Meaning	Examples in English
ab	away from	abstract, abstain, abolish
acri	bitter	acrid, acrimony, exacerbate
ambi	both	ambiguous, ambidextrous, ambivalent
aud	hear	auditory, audition, audience
bene	good	beneficial, benign, benevolent
circum	around	circumstance, circumference, circumvent
dict	say	dictate, diction, dictionary
form	shape	conform, reform, formulate
jur	law	jury, justice, justify
luc	light	lucid, elucidate, translucent
mal	evil/wrong	malevolent, malpractice, malediction
mort	death	mortality, immortal, mortify
omni	all	omniscient, omnipotent, omnipresent
pac	peace	pacifist, pacify, pacification
sens	feeling	sensitive, sentient, resentment
vac	empty	vacuous, vacuum, evacuate
vis	see	invisible, vivid, visage

Punctuation

Type	Symbol	Effect
Full stop/period	.	Mark the end of a sentence and can be used to create sentence fragments and lots of short, sharp sentences for drama.
Comma	,	Separates items in a list or clauses in a sentence to ensure smooth reading and prevent ambiguity. The Oxford comma (the comma before 'and' at the end of a list) is optional but can help add clarity (e.g. 'We played Uno, Scrabble, and Snakes and Ladders').
Apostrophe	'	Indicates possession (e.g. Myra's book) or contraction (e.g. wouldn't).
Question mark	?	Indicates an interrogative sentence that poses a question.
Exclamation mark	!	Adds emphasis and conveys extreme/heightened emotions e.g. surprise, excitement, aggression, elation.
Colon	:	Introduces explanations or lists, creating a sense of expectation.
Semicolon	;	Combines two independent clauses to more closely unite two ideas (e.g. I studied hard for this exam; I think I'm going to pass.). Note that these can't be dependent clauses (e.g. I studied hard for this exam; so that I can pass.) The two clauses on either side of the semicolon need to work as standalone sentences.
Parenthesis/brackets	( )	Enclose additional information or clarification. This can make text feel more precise if the parenthetical information adds detail, or feel more conversational if the parentheticals are more like extra remarks.
Dash	-	Creates a stronger break than a comma, adding emphasis, interruption, or an abrupt change in tone.
Quotation marks	" "	Indicate direct speech. These can be 'single' or "double quote marks" (just pick one and be consistent).
Ellipsis	...	Suggests hesitation, omission, or trailing thoughts, adding suspense or ambiguity.

Common punctuation mistakes

Apostrophes
- If a noun is plural, the apostrophe goes after the 's' at the end (e.g. *The girl's book* = one girl owns the book; *The girls' book* = multiple girls own the book).
- If a name ends with an 's', you can either write the apostrophe and add an extra 's' or leave it out – either option is fine, but pick one and be consistent (e.g. *Doris' sewing machine* or *Doris's sewing machine*).
- Use possessive apostrophes even if it is not a person doing the possessing (e.g. *in two years' time, today's date, a day's work*).
- If you have a collective plural like *children* or *people,* then add a *'s* like normal (e.g. children's and people's, not childrens' or peoples').
- You do not need apostrophes to indicate normal plural words (e.g. The dog's were playing)

Its vs. it's
- <u>Its</u> without an apostrophe shows possession (e.g. the dog ate its breakfast). <u>It's</u> is a contraction for *it is* (e.g. it's breakfast time!).
- To tell the two apart, try replacing it with the words 'it is' – if that works, then you need the apostrophe.

Comma splicing
- A comma splice is when two independent clauses (complete sentences) are incorrectly joined by a comma instead of a full stop. This creates a run-on sentence that lacks the proper conjunction or punctuation to separate ideas clearly. E.g. 'I love reading, I find it very relaxing.' or 'The day was over, we had to go home.'
- To fix comma splices, you can:
  - Replace the comma with a full stop to create two separate sentences (ideal if the sentence is already long). E.g. I love reading. I find it very relaxing.
  - Remove the comma and use a conjunction (ideal if you want to clarify the relationship between the two ideas) E.g. The day was over so we had to go home.
  - Use a semicolon and a conjunction (ideal if you want to add formality and sophistication). E.g. The day was over; therefore, we had to go home.

Grammar

Word classes

- **Nouns:** refer to people, places, or things.
  - You can test whether a word is a noun by seeing if it fits the blank in the sentence: *'Can you please give me ___?'* (e.g. the pen, happiness, dinosaurs).
  - **Proper nouns** refer to the names of people or places (e.g. Queen Elizabeth II, Neptune, Manchester).
  - **Pronouns** replace nouns in sentences (e.g. I, me, my, we, our, you, your, he, his, her, hers, they, them, their, it, its).

- **Adjectives:** are describing words that tell us something about a noun.
  - You can test whether a word is an adjective by seeing if it fits the blank in the sentence: 'I love my ___ car' (e.g. red, fast, expensive).
  - Adjectives can also stack on top of each other, so we can get long phrases like 'I love my twelve, amazing, big, new, red, electric cars.' There are grammatical rules about the order of these adjectives – for example, it would sound weird to say 'I love my electric, red, big car.'
  - Adjectives are almost always optional, meaning we can remove them and the sentence still makes sense (e.g. 'I love my car.').

- **Prepositions:** are words that express a relationship between two things (e.g. to, on, before).

- **Conjunctions:** are linking words (e.g. FANBOYS: for, and, nor, but, or, yet, so). There are also more complex ones like similarly, furthermore, likewise, whereas, although, etc.

- **Verbs:** are action words and something you can 'do'.
  - You can test whether a word is a verb I want to ___ on Tuesday' (e.g. go, succeed, cook).
  - Verbs often end in '-ing' for present tense or '-ed' for past tense. (e.g. going, succeeded, cooking).

- **Adverbs:** are describing words that tell us something about a verb.
  - You can test whether a word is an adjective by seeing if it fits the blank in the sentence: 'I walked ___ to class.' (e.g. quickly, quietly, happily).
  - Adverbs almost always end in '-ly', and generally give us more information about the way something happened.
  - Like adjectives, adverbs are optional and can be removed while still leaving us with a complete sentence (e.g. 'I walked to class.') They can also sit at the edge of sentences separated by commas to indicate they are saying something about the overall sentence (e.g. 'Unfortunately, I lost the bet').

- **Articles:** refer to the words a, an, and the that come before nouns.
  - The words a and an are **indefinite articles** because they don't have to refer to one specific thing. For instance, if I say 'I want to go to a party,' you wouldn't know which party I was talking about.
  - The word the is a **definite article** because it refers to something specific. For instance, if I say 'I want to go to the party,' you would know that I was talking about one particular party, and not just any party.

Grammar

Clauses and sentence fragments

In English, standard sentences must contain a **main clause** consisting of a noun phrase and a verb phrase in that specific order. They can have a whole bunch of other things too, but those two components have to be there.

E.g. noun phrases and verb phrases:

- I travelled a lot in my youth.
- Fred was too old to jump on the trampoline.
- Because I handed in my essay late, my English teacher yelled at me.
- My mother, in her infinite wisdom, decided to enrol me in ballet classes.

Some of the information in these sentences is optional – we could just say 'I travelled' and 'my English teacher yelled at me' and we'd still have a grammatical sentence. We can also have other optional information separating the noun phrase from the verb phrase. However, we can't leave out the noun phrases or verb phrases. These are the two essential parts of the sentence!

When either a noun phrase or a verb phrase is missing, we end up with a sentence fragment, which means the sentence is incomplete.

For example, the underlined sentences below are fragments:

Throughout the novel, the theme of family becomes increasingly important. Signifying how the author believes family to be a valuable force in helping people overcome trauma. Rosey struggles with her traumatic past, but she conquers this with the help of her parents and siblings. Her father Rob, who loses his job, and her mother Dianne, who wants a divorce, as well as her two brothers. Each character experiences loss, but the novel shows how they become united and are made stronger by their struggles. For example, her brother and his alcoholism. Therefore, suggesting that family plays a vital role in our lives.

In formal and analytical writing, you should always fix sentence fragments. The only exception to this is in imaginative writing as there are more flexible rules when writing dialogue or stream-of-consciousness inner monologues.

Subject and object

- The **subject** is the agent of the sentence (which is the person or thing *doing* the verb).
- The **object** is the thing that the verb affects.
- Sentences can either be **active** (subject-focused) or **passive** (object-focused). Both kinds of sentences are completely grammatical, but you may want to use one or the other depending on whether you want to focus on the subject or the object. For example:
  - **Active:** The author tells readers that tourism numbers will increase.
  - **Passive:** The readers are told by the author that tourism numbers will increase.
- We can also write **agentless passive** sentences that omit the subject (e.g. 'The readers are told that tourism numbers will increase.'). This can be useful to avoid repetition, but it is also something you can analyse as writers may use this deliberately in order to distract from who the subject is (e.g. 'Speaking up in class is prohibited.' → 'The teacher is prohibiting speaking up in class!')

Grammar

Types of sentences

Type		Definition	Example	Effect
Declarative		A statement or 'normal' sentence with a subject and verb, ending with a full stop. These can be simple, compound, complex, or compound-complex.	"I am Ozymandias."	Conveys straightforward information and can be imbued with any tone (e.g. factual, nostalgic, argumentative) depending on the length, diction, and context.
	Simple	A declarative sentence with just one independent clause (i.e. a subject + verb), typically a short sentence.	"Thought is free."	Present information unambiguously, conveying certainty or absolute truth. Short, simple sentences can also be used to vary the rhythm and flow of a passage.
Declarative	Compound	Two independent clauses joined by a conjunction (remember FANBOYS: for, and, nor, but, or, yet, so).	"Hell is empty <u>and</u> all the devils are here."	Creates an association between two ideas which can suggest a cause-and-effect relationship or a relationship of similarity or contrast.
	Complex	One independent clause plus one or more dependent clauses (i.e. phrases that can't be a standalone sentence) that starts with a subordinating conjunction (e.g. although, while, because).	"<u>When</u> he shall die, Take him and cut him out in little stars"	Add depth, nuance, and associations to otherwise simple statements, allowing an author to explore more sophisticated ideas. Combining these into compound-complex sentences further allows an author to write longer sentences that convey more intricacies or interconnectedness than simple sentences can.
Imperative		A command or request that begins with a verb and is directed at a person.	"Get thee to a nunnery!"	Convey authority, control, urgency, desperation, or certainty. Typically these statements come across as either forceful/demanding or pleading/despairing.
Interrogative		A question statement ending in a question mark. This could be a real question or a rhetorical one.	"Is this a dagger which I see before me?"	Provoke contemplation and reflection when directed at the audience, or express curiosity, uncertainty, or apprehension when used as character dialogue.
Exclamative		Express strong emotion and end with an exclamation mark. These may be single words or sentence fragments, also known as interjections.	"O Romeo, Romeo!"	Heighten emotional intensity and emphasise extreme feeling – this could be anything: surprise, joy, rage, longing, etc.
Conditional/ hypothetical		Uses words like 'if' or 'unless' to describe a possibility or something that depends on a certain condition.	"If you prick us, do we not bleed?"	Encourage readers to consider a possible scenario and contemplate hypothetical circumstances in order to make a point
Elliptical		A sentence that omits information, sometimes with the use of an ellipsis (…) or other times with concise grammar.	"She loves him, and he her"	Reduces unnecessary words or phrases to distil an idea down to its most simple or elegant expression, or to leave unspoken ideas and emotions implied.

Vocabulary

Replacement words to use instead of...

Below are some commonly overused words in English Language with synonyms you can use instead to give your writing more variety and specificity.
- **SHOWS:** demonstrates, portrays, reveals, clarifies, illustrates, depicts, explains, accentuates, emphasises, underlines, highlights, underscores, elucidates
- **SUGGESTS:** implies, connotes, signifies, symbolises, represents, hints, engenders, reflects, conveys, reiterates, supports, explicates
- **SAYS:** asserts, claims, states, declares, argues, explains, emphasises, expresses, proclaims, communicates
- **GOOD:** admirable, commendable, noteworthy, benevolent, impressive, virtuous, praiseworthy, exemplary
- **BAD:** detrimental, flawed, harmful, ineffective, inferior, unfavorable, deficient, problematic, reprehensible, deplorable, malevolent
- **IMPORTANT:** pivotal, crucial, essential, fundamental, significant, core, vital, integral, key, paramount, indispensable
- **VERY:** extremely, exceptionally, incredibly, tremendously, profoundly, remarkably, overwhelmingly, intensely, hugely, significantly

Words to describe tone

Positive:
- Optimistic
- Joyful
- Hopeful
- Lighthearted
- Enthusiastic
- Inspirational
- Affectionate
- Warm
- Playful
- Encouraging

Negative:
- Melancholic
- Gloomy
- Cynical
- Bitter
- Pessimistic
- Mournful
- Despondent
- Resigned
- Harsh
- Depressing

Humorous and ironic:
- Witty
- Satirical
- Sardonic
- Amusing
- Playful
- Joking
- Mocking
- Clever
- Parodic
- Irreverent

Sentimental:
- Romantic
- Nostalgic
- Tender
- Passionate
- Affectionate
- Dreamy
- Poignant
- Loving
- Sensual
- Lyrical

Philosophical:
- Reflective
- Meditative
- Thoughtful
- Contemplative
- Pensive
- Intellectual
- Profound
- Solemn
- Rational
- Speculative

Neutral:
- Formal
- Informative
- Objective
- Factual
- Concise
- Measured
- Calm
- Analytical
- Instructive
- Pragmatic

Angry and critical:
- Hostile
- Sarcastic
- Contemptuous
- Scornful
- Outraged
- Furious
- Accusatory
- Condescending
- Disdainful
- Reproachful

Dark and mysterious:
- Ominous
- Foreboding
- Sinister
- Haunting
- Eerie
- Mysterious
- Macabre
- Grim
- Suspenseful
- Unsettling

Dramatic and intense:
- Urgent
- Tense
- Exaggerated
- Bombastic
- Grandiose
- Emotional
- Overwrought
- Vehement
- Theatrical
- Forceful

Imaginative:
- Surreal
- Fantastical
- Quirky
- Dreamlike
- Enchanting
- Magical
- Playful
- Whimsical
- Eccentric
- Mythical

Vocabulary

High-level vocabulary

Expanding your vocabulary can enhance clarity, precision, and depth in your writing. However, high-level words should be used with caution as misusing them can make your writing confusing or unnatural. To build and apply your vocabulary effectively, read widely to see how these words are used in context. For this word list, look up definitions to determine if a word is likely to be useful to you. You can then include these on flashcards or just annotate this page and keep it open next time you're writing an essay! Integrate words carefully the first time, and always seek feedback from your teacher to make sure you're using them correctly!

A
- Abstruse
- Acquiesce
- Adroit
- Alacrity
- Ameliorate
- Anachronistic
- Anathema
- Apocryphal
- Approbation
- Assiduous

B
- Bellicose
- Benign
- Bequeath
- Bombastic
- Bucolic
- Buttress
- Byzantine
- Blithe
- Bereft
- Bifurcate

C
- Cajole
- Capricious
- Castigate
- Chicanery
- Circumlocution
- Cogent
- Conflagration
- Conundrum
- Corroborate
- Culpable

D
- Deleterious
- Demagogue
- Desultory
- Diatribe
- Dichotomy
- Didactic
- Diffident
- Disparate
- Dissonance
- Dogmatic

E
- Ebullient
- Effulgent
- Elucidate
- Enervate
- Ennui
- Ephemeral
- Equanimity
- Esoteric
- Evanescent
- Exacerbate

F
- Fastidious
- Fatuous
- Fecund
- Flippant
- Fortuitous
- Frenetic
- Furtive
- Fulminate
- Facetious
- Feckless

G
- Garrulous
- Grandiloquent
- Gregarious
- Guile
- Gumption
- Gossamer
- Gratuitous
- Germane
- Galvanise
- Gainsay

H
- Harangue
- Haughty
- Hedonistic
- Hegemony
- Histrionic
- Homogeneous
- Hubris
- Hyperbole
- Hypothetical
- Heretical

I
- Iconoclast
- Ignominious
- Illicit
- Imbroglio
- Impetuous
- Incendiary
- Inchoate
- Ineffable
- Inimical
- Inscrutable

J
- Juxtaposition
- Jingoistic
- Jettison
- Jocund
- Jocular
- Jejune
- Jubilant
- Judicious
- Jurisprudence
- Jargon

K
- Kowtow
- Kafkaesque
- Kudos
- Kernel
- Kinetic
- Kindle
- Knell
- Keenly
- Knack
- Knavish

L
- Laconic
- Languid
- Largesse
- Latent
- Lethargic
- Loquacious
- Lugubrious
- Licentious
- Lurid
- Labyrinthine

M
- Maelstrom
- Magnanimous
- Mendacious
- Mellifluous
- Mercurial
- Misanthropic
- Mitigate
- Mollify
- Myopic
- Munificent

N
- Nefarious
- Nescient
- Nonchalant
- Noxious
- Nuance
- Nebulous
- Niggling
- Nonplussed
- Nomenclature
- Nascent

O
- Obfuscate
- Obsequious
- Onerous
- Ostentatious
- Opaque
- Omniscient
- Oracular
- Opulent
- Overwrought
- Oblivious

P
- Paradigm
- Parsimonious
- Pejorative
- Pernicious
- Perspicacious
- Pervasive
- Phlegmatic
- Platitude
- Prodigious
- Pugnacious

Q
- Quixotic
- Quagmire
- Querulous
- Quizzical
- Quiescent
- Quintessential
- Quotidian
- Quell
- Qualm
- Quibble

R
- Reified
- Recalcitrant
- Recondite
- Redolent
- Refulgent
- Resplendent
- Reticent
- Rhapsodic
- Ribald
- Rueful

S
- Sagacious
- Sanguine
- Scrupulous
- Soporific
- Spurious
- Stentorian
- Supercilious
- Surreptitious
- Sycophant
- Synthesis

T
- Tautological
- Temerity
- Tenebrous
- Truculent
- Truncated
- Trepidation
- Turgid
- Terse
- Transient
- Tantamount

U
- Ubiquitous
- Umbrage
- Unctuous
- Undulate
- Unequivocal
- Unilateral
- Untenable
- Uxorious
- Upbraid
- Usurp

V
- Vacillate
- Variegated
- Vehement
- Veracity
- Verdant
- Vicarious
- Vindicate
- Vitriolic
- Volition
- Voracious

W
- Wane
- Wanton
- Wistful
- Winsome
- Wizened
- Wheedle
- Waggish
- Wraith
- Wayward
- Wry

X
- Xenophobic
- Xanthic
- Xenomorphic

Y
- Yeoman
- Yoke
- Yonder
- Yearn
- Yielding

Z
- Zealot
- Zenith
- Zephyr
- Zeitgeist
- Zoetic